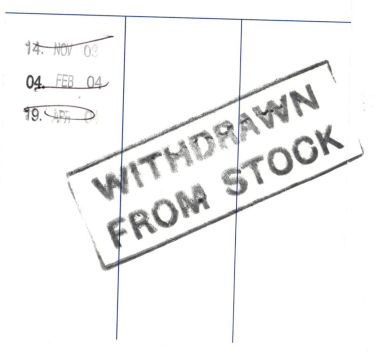

A
Haven
for
Childhood

The building
of a
Steiner Kindergarten

by
Christopher Day

STARBORN BOOKS

STARBORN BOOKS
A HAVEN FOR CHILDHOOD
The building of a Steiner Kindergarten
by
Christopher Day

First published 1998 by STARBORN BOOKS
© Starborn Books 1998

ISBN 1 899530 05 3

British Library Cataloguing in Publication Data

A catalogue record for this book is available from
the British Library

727.1 DAY

STARBORN BOOKS
Glanrhydwilym, Rhydwilym, Clunderwen, Carmarthenshire,
UK

CONTENTS

Foreword:
A Teacher's Perspective

by Anita de Vries

Coming from the flattest and most densely populated part of Holland, I was very lucky to be offered a job as kindergarten teacher in this very beautiful part of South-West Wales. I began work in a very small classroom incorporated into the main school building, but with promises of a bright future in the soon-to-be-completed new kindergarten building across the road. Chris Day and numerous voluntary work parties, both local and from across Europe, had been working on this project for a few years by this time, but the kindergarten finally opened for the first group of children in the summer of 1991.

A magical environment had been created, especially designed for the youngest children in our school. The rounded and womb-like form of the two classrooms make most children, even on their first day, feel secure and at home. It has been a privilege to work in a building where so much thought and care have been given to all aspects of early childhood. The soft forms of room and alcoves within, the warmth of natural wood, used from floors to carved door-latches, the subdued lighting - all these give a welcoming feeling to child and visitor alike.

I remember the delivery man who happened to be dropping off some parcels for the school. He could not help but be drawn inside, amazed that this was not an artist's flight of fancy but an actual place of work and play. "I wish," he sighed, "I could be a child again!"

Surrounded as it is by forest, field and river, the kindergarten has been perfectly blended into its environment. Looking down upon it from the top of our school field, no one would guess that those two little grass hillocks with a chimney tucked in between is the home of the first steps of our children's education, their haven of peace in this world full of pressure and the drive for achievement.

Anita de Vries, Nant-y-Cwm, 1998.

Chapter 1
Background:
The Steiner School Movement

The kindergarten at Nant-y-Cwm must be seen in the context of the Waldorf educational movement. This goes back to 1919, when the director of the Waldorf cigarette company in Stuttgart asked Rudolf Steiner if he could help set up a school for the factory workers' children. Steiner recommended a draft curriculum. He also selected and trained teachers, although much of this 'training' was in the form of cultivating insight into the human being and the child's journey towards adulthood.

To support inner freedom in the individual, the education is based upon bringing into balance *thinking* (and rationality), *feeling* (and morality) and *the will* (and practicality). Hence every aspect of the education is permeated by ethical values, artistic feeling and physical experience. Steiner observed that children pass through certain stages of development, both inwardly and physically. In the first seven years, more or less, every cell in the body has been renewed. At the end of this time, the teeth start to be replaced. During these years, the relationship of children to the world is primarily through activity. They imitate rather than understand. In the next seven years, leading up to puberty, they are led very much by feelings. Only in the post-puberty, third seven-year period, can they properly cope with abstract intellectual learning - though, as for any adult, the less abstract, the more experiential and the more inspiring (hence ethically related, and artistically soul-connecting) the better. Both *what* is taught, and at least as importantly, *how* it is taught, take account of this and other, subtler development patterns.

From this first school in Stuttgart grew the Steiner School movement. In the UK and many other countries, the schools are often called 'Waldorf Schools' after its beginnings. In 1936 all Waldorf schools in Germany were closed by the Nazis - who did not appreciate an education that encouraged people to think for themselves and strengthened resistance to manipulation. Many teachers, and others active in work Steiner had inspired, fled abroad, so exporting the ideas upon which the Waldorf movement is founded.

In 1944 the original school was bombed by the British, but since the war, and especially in recent decades, the movement has blossomed. There are now some six hundred schools world wide, from Siberia, Japan and India to North and South America; from Scandinavia to Africa and Australasia. They share common ground in their understanding of the human being, yet each one is unique in context, culture and social individuality - and this gives individual flavour to each school, and its buildings. Nant-y-Cwm Steiner School in Wales is one of them.

Chapter 2
Before the Kindergarten:
Nant-y-Cwm Steiner School

In one way, Nant-y-Cwm Steiner School was a mistake. Nobody had thought of building a Steiner school, but events made it happen.

It all started with Bio-dynamic farming. At meetings connected with this agricultural movement in the mid 1970s, various families interested in Steiner education, but dispersed across West Wales, began to come into contact with one another. A common concern emerged: as there were no Steiner schools in the area, some families felt compelled to move to England when their children reached school age. Others would stay, but were saddened that there would be no Steiner education for their children.

Amongst the activities arranged were a demonstration kindergarten weekend, lectures on child-development and education and even a home-school for one child, by an ex-Waldorf teacher. But this was all - until one lecturer suggested that we start our own Saturday play-school, to bring to children activities absent from their conventional school experience.

We did, and its success was rapid. Staffed by parents, it grew to some 28 children, at a cost of 50p per child per morning, usually plus food and help. This we held in a friend's house, but her husband became ill, so the play-school moved to another house. This family had marital difficulties, so it moved again. By now some parents had lost track of where to find the next session and the disruptions were affecting the children.

We started to look for more permanent premises. Schoolrooms were expensive to rent. Village halls were set up for play-groups and after each session we had to return every item of plastic equipment to its exact former position - no chance to create the atmosphere we felt essential. But one of our number saw an advertisement for a school for sale. He rang me up but I thought it a mad idea. We had no pupils for a school, no teachers, no money... Maybe in three or four years, but not now.

The upshot was that a group went to see it. In the pre-dusk gloom and drizzle of a November afternoon, it looked depressing, if not haunted. In the twenty years it had been empty, only a few windows had been broken, only one hole had appeared in the roof, but the cinder playground was full of wrecked cars, the interior was decorated with Dracula graffiti, and floor, roof and wainscot had patches of rotten timber.

Inspecting the roof, we nearly lost a teenager. Against advice, he stepped on the ceiling and disappeared. There was a heart-stopping crash of wreckage hitting the piled broken furniture on the floor sixteen feet below, then silence. To my relief, a head slowly appeared from the hole - he had been able to grab the joists as he fell.

The school cost £6,500 to buy - which gives an idea of its condition! And we must indeed have been mad, for we bought it. For speed, two families loaned the money for subsequent transfer to the school as soon as it became a legal entity. This in fact took several years, during which we converted it and brought it into use. Technically, over this period, the private owners were profiting from all the gifts, in work, money and kind, that went into renovation. A 'scandal' fortunately never exposed by the press.

The group - although legally only consisting of the two families - was now the owner of a derelict school building, useless until repaired and converted. It had no electricity or gas. Water was in a well with a seized hand-pump. Windows were too high even for adults to see out of and there were only two classrooms and a small kitchen, built a year or so before the school was closed in the 1950s. The only trace of toilets was a hole in the ground over a leaky-jointed drain that passed about five feet from the well, though twenty feet above water level, on its way to discharge half-way down the cliff above the river. The next door house shared this drain, so the outlet was clearly advertised by a long stream of toilet paper.

With all energies diverted to the 'proper' school in the offing, the playgroup wound itself up. Full of optimism about what we thought an excellent idea - the first Steiner school in Wales - we approached everyone we could think of for money. Not a single penny did this raise.

After six months, we realised we were faced with a stark choice: sell up - no doubt at a loss - giving up for ever the idea of a school, or start work, even though we did not have any money, and see what would happen. We chose to start.

We did not *quite* have no money. A barn dance had raised some, and by a mistake never repeated, the non-profit making playgroup had actually made a profit. This totalled £36 and some pence - equalling, in those days, ten bags of cement *or* a load of sand, not both. So we started on those jobs that did *not* cost any money, like digging foundation holes, without being able to afford the concrete to go in them. We also lowered windows to a more inviting level.

The school opened temporarily in the former village post-office. Naively optimistic, we planned to open the 'proper' school two terms later. Miraculously, we did so, but not in a finished building.

No sooner had we started, than help began to come to us - much from people with nothing to gain; some had no school-age children, others who raised money for us, lived hundreds of miles away. We had an anonymous donation for £1,000 from the USA; a pound was slipped under the door into the building rubble. And there were other unexpected boosts to morale, like the concert soloist who played to the volunteer builders in the draughty, rain-lashed, windowless building.

This was an inspiring time, but it was also humbling as we became aware that higher beings were helping us from invisible realms. It seemed as though the effort of will to overcome physical obstacles and threats to morale unlocked a channel for these forces.

The obstacles were great. Hardly any money - which often meant soul-destroying work: mixing huge volumes of concrete by hand - hours instead of minutes with a mixer; days digging in the rain instead of JCB minutes, taking apart rotten second-hand trusses to use the timber, straightening nails. Ecologically desirable perhaps, but unremitting drudgery for the few individuals who had to do it. The mismatch of construction sequence and season forced by scant monetary and human resources, together with my management inexperience, and everyone's lack of skill made work hard, but never quite too daunting. We had for instance, no alternative but to lay drains in hard frost, when plastic (sorry! I wouldn't use it now) is more brittle and gravel beds had to be levelled with a pickaxe. We built the cesspool in the winter, with water level rising nightly faster than construction. The pump we resorted to filled the excavation with noise and exhaust smoke. One volunteer steadied himself on freshly laid blocks and fell in. What luck it was only water in the cesspool, and only four feet deep.

There was more to do than just repair the roof and add drains and toilets. Central to Steiner education is the recognition that as children develop their needs progress, so they must be taught in separate age-group classes. This means separate classrooms. There were two already, but this would only be adequate for the opening year. Three more would be needed. To accommodate these, space could be found in the roof, but joists and ground-floor ceilings would have to go in now. Floors could follow in due course.

Eventually, after ten months' work and £4,239 expenditure, we were able to open the school at Michaelmas 1979. There were now toilets, electricity, water, wood-stove heating and two almost completed classrooms. One of these was divided by a temporary screen, of negligible sound-

To bring classrooms more down to a child scale, we sloped the ceiling edges and corners down, while the centres rise to give vertical breathing space and upward posture induction.

proofing value, to make a third classroom, just usable, albeit with difficulty. Like all temporary things, this lasted for several years. The ceiling above had no floor over it. During the laying of that, a foot came through into the classroom below - much to the children's delight, but not to anybody else's, especially not to the foot's owner's.

Chaos, crisis, discomfort and sweat. But nonetheless, something apparently impossible had come into existence - and that on a shoestring budget, barely one seventh of normal prices. Looking back to that apparently lunatic decision to buy the uninhabitable building some eighteen months previously, it became clear to us that our actions in the world of hard, intractable matter had enabled something spiritual to come into being, something that had been waiting for us to start, to sacrifice and struggle, to *do*. I am continually reminded of Goethe's words:

"Whatever you can do, or dream you can, begin it.
Boldness has genius, power and magic in it."

The school was now open, but by no means finished. As children progressed through the classes it would, moreover, need an additional classroom each year for the next three years. But with the school now actually in being, the urgency was no longer so visible. Volunteer numbers dropped to one or two and work in the gloomy, unlit roof-space dragged slowly. These upstairs rooms needed windows, which meant holes in the roof. Sure enough as soon as we had fully opened them up, we were caught by rain, but managed, with some personal risk, to brave tarpaulin-tugging winds and slippery scaffolding to improvise temporary covers. Building a classroom over the former kitchen meant demolishing its asbestos roof and supporting gable wall. In doing so, we unknowingly damaged cables fixed to this, narrowly escaping burning the building down. This was only one of the communication problems involving electricity. Over the years there were six volunteer electricians, most of whom fixed cables for subsequent connection, but then left the job before doing so. None left notes and each used a different cable marking system. Eventually however, the chaos became classrooms, but not before disorder and mess had started to affect the children.

New teachers, who had not shared the struggles and improvisation of the early days, felt that the voluntary approach to building, with its slow rate of completion and consequent prolonged construction mess, was too disruptive an influence on the children. It had served its purpose, but now should stop. Two professionals were employed to finish a classroom, but the money ran out before they completed it. We now had the difficult task of rebuilding volunteer morale. Equally hard, was the fact that all the simple tasks had been done, leaving only those too complicated and skilled for most volunteers. Normally I would work ahead on these so as to have jobs suitable to the skills of whoever came to help. And of course, there was no money left for materials; and the frustrations about slow completion were more intense than ever. Those were not easy days.

It was with considerable relief that we finished the last classroom. At around £81 per sq metre (1985 prices including VAT) it had cost about 13% of comparable school buildings, but this takes no account of the sweat and stress. Stress in particular I was glad to have behind me. Now, at last, my volunteer building days were over - or so I thought. No more drudgery due to lack of equipment. No more desperate improvisation with barely suitable materials. No more hand-stiffening, skin-cracking work in winter rain and mud, just because help and monetary backup was unpredictable.

But this was not to be.

Chapter 3
The new Kindergarten:
the Building Story

Small as our original aspirations may have been, over the years the school grew. Space became tighter and tighter, eventually inadequate. Rather than extending the existing building to make new classrooms, we decided to build a completely separate kindergarten, so protecting small children from the robustness of older play - a twelve-year old can run a hundred feet looking backwards: woe betide anyone in the way. Moreover we could create a special realm with atmosphere matched to this age group, wonder-filled and open to everything around them. But where should it be? What should it be like?

A parent donated a plot of land. As overgrown woodland, it had no obvious starting point to grow from. A group of us walked around the site, trying to sense where a building would feel right. The steep slope to the river and the need to protect child-realm from road, narrowed the choice to the level edge-strip. The dynamic energy concentrated at the road-bend invited transformation into upward gesture, human activity and built form. Here would grow the building.

But how big? I asked the kindergarten teacher. How did she use her present room? Was it big enough? What did a kindergarten need? She described how entry into wider society is often daunting for small children. Going to school is a big first step. For many children, kindergarten is their first real consistent social experience. A regular part of every

Steiner kindergarten school-day therefore includes games of a social nature. Many of these are 'ring-games', drawing on the sociability engendered by circle-based dispositions and movements. We decided, therefore, to make each room a circle equal in area to her kindergarten room. Being cautious, I subsequently enlarged this, though in the event not quite enough.

The rhythm of the school day, like breathing, alternates between the inward-focussed, tightly-structured, and the expansive and free. For free play, children need places to play in where their imagination is unhindered. Typically, they seek out corner-like semi-enclosures. Circles of course don't have corners, but set within (more or less) squares, they do.

The geometry of a cone on a (more or less) square with rounded corners, gives low-ceilinged corner nooks as play alcoves. The plan of each room, therefore, is a sort of 'circle-with-corners', so while each classroom retains a circular quality, its shape is in fact much more variegated.

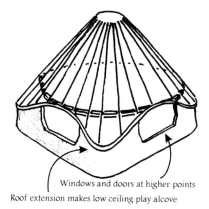

Windows and doors at higher points

Roof extension makes low ceiling play alcove

With the supporting facilities linking the two classrooms and forming a roadside noise screen, the basic form was now established. All agreed the building should be child-scaled and welcoming, but a slate roof, locally traditional, would need to be steep, so unduly imposing; cedar would not last long under dripping trees and all low-slope materials had an industrial appearance and would rigidify the form - except for a vegetated roof. This became the obvious choice.

We felt it important both that the building should blend seamlessly with its surroundings, and that its atmosphere and aura should be appropriate to the children's needs. Hence its form should arise out of these considerations, not imitate vernacular precedents or associate with any particular style.

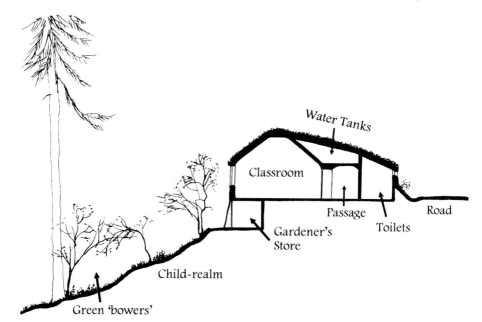

But what would the planners think? We invited the planning officer to the school and showed him round. By the time we came to discuss our design, his initial scepticsm had disappeared. He observed that our proposed kindergarten was on a separate plot of land from the main school building, across the road and nearly a hundred yards away. Were it within the curtilage, this would be no problem; indeed he would like to see more such buildings. Fortunately, however, there was no definition of curtilage, so he was free to decide that it would include this plot.

Building regulations proved a bigger problem, one I had not anticipated as I thought I had met all requirements. The building control officer did not agree. In his view, the building would fall down without a central post and, for good measure, a reinforced concrete ring-beam. A post would make the room unusable, and I foresaw thermal, condensation and leakage problems with a concrete ring-beam the whole width of the wall. Cast by volunteers a bit at a time, the problems would be even worse. Anyway, with a central post, what need for a ring-beam - and visa versa. My structural engineer said the design was sound, the council's engineer said it was not, but for months they were not allowed to talk directly to each other, only correspond via myself and building control. As we could not delay, we started construction while this wrangling was still going on. After twenty-three months, with the roof constructed and not falling down, the engineers were allowed to talk directly to each other and we were grudgingly granted permission.

From the economic standpoint, volunteer building was the only option. But should we wait for the appeal to bring in money? No money was in sight, so we decided just to go ahead anyway, before enthusiasm faded. It was now autumn. With winter coming: not the best time for excavation and outdoor work.

Building started with a flurry of enthusiasm. We cleared sufficient ground to mark out the building - but not too much to upset the spirit of place, no more than was essential. Then we built a site-hut from trees and offcut slab-wood. None of this cost anything. At a bargain-cheap weekend rate, we hired a JCB, tractor and trailer to excavate. The tractor and trailer never appeared, so before long all the setting-out marks, pegs and strings were buried under spoil. So much for penny-pinching. One family donated the cost of ready-mix foundation concrete. This was delivered by conveyor boom, swinging wildly about the site at waist height, while helpers and children jumped out of the way or ducked into trenches.

For a brief few months, two of us were paid £1.75 an hour as core workers to prepare for and supervise volunteers. My colleague had interesting habits, like 'borrowing' insulation already placed in wall cavities; moreover he was somewhat accident prone. This culminated in him catching his finger in a hydraulic crane-grab during a concrete block delivery. By some miracle his finger survived but the experience was sobering for everyone.

Work in those early days was enlivened by violent rows between one volunteer, his ex-wife and pregnant ex-girlfriend. On top of this, we were working in winter, in mud, rain, snow and frost, sometimes having to use a pickaxe - with eyes closed against icy chips - to open the frozen sand-heap. We mixed concrete by hand, only later getting a mixer, so stomach-strainingly frustrating to start and with such clouds of foul exhaust smoke when it did work, that hand-mixing often seemed preferable. It wasn't easy, but working on curves seemed to be energising, whereas straight lined rectangles are energy draining. Moreover, the location was beautiful, the river sang nearby and, as we worked as late as daylight allowed, owls would regularly hoot and screech around us as we washed up tools in the dark. To draw water for this, we had to feel with our feet for the river edge. No-one quite fell in. I enjoyed those times.

Volunteer numbers were highly variable. In most periods there was usually one 'regular' besides myself, and sometimes several others, sometimes none. I had learnt to always work ahead on all the complicated and unrewarding fiddles so as to have jobs ready should unexpected extra helpers turn up -

but tasks and tools were stretched to the limit when about twelve 'convoy' travellers appeared. Their initially aggressive manner rapidly mellowed and they not only did a lot, but were good company.

Whereas surroundings of unremitting straight lines sap energy, those made up of curves re-invigorate. Curves are not only more restful to the eye, but seem to give energy to those who work with them.

More difficult was keeping the job going when money was low, and simultaneously fending off the teachers' frustration with our slow progress. At the beginning, Kenneth Bayes had prepared an appeal booklet but, for all its professional quality, it brought in very little money, and so, for two periods of several months each, I was suddenly instructed to limit expenditure to £5 a month. To maintain momentum when there might be wood but no nails, or cement and lime but no sand or blocks was difficult enough. With the frustrations of urgency unabated, it was personally wearing. In between these lean times, some selected volunteers were suddenly paid £1 an hour to speed things up, and I tried to survive the pressures of a stop-go life.

Several manfacturers offered generous discounts on materials, although some, like wood preservatives or radioactive insulation blocks, we thought unsuitable and so did not take up. Dennis Ruabon gave us quarry tiles and Emlyn Brick Co. paving bricks. Nonetheless, finances continued to be desperately tight and the cause of much stress.

We held several workshops on the theme of building as an artistic process. These were structured to balance physical work with artistic and cultural activities, feeding the feelings and thinking as well as the body. They needed months of preparation as we aimed to give the opportunity to experience marked change in a bare week. Unlike similar workshops at the main school in the 70s, we had only around three or four participants, and one year even had to cancel. Gift-work and practical experience seemed weak in appeal in Britain in the 80s. But we did have help from overseas. Two Dutchmen came to work with us, each for several months. One - a skilled carpenter - complete with a converted lorry, full of family. Over an intense two weeks some twenty-five sixteen year olds,

Class Eleven of a Swedish Waldorf school, turfed the roof and rendered most of the inside walls - some becoming skilled hand-plasterers in the process.

Nine-year-olds in every Waldorf school do a four week block of practical building as one of their 'Main Lesson' blocks. One year, children from Nant-y-Cwm did this on the kindergarten site. The wall they built went up so fast, it was hard to keep it corrected for verticality. With them, I used the same teamwork techniques by which unskilled volunteers support, rather than obstruct each other. For block-laying, for example, one person lays mortar, one sets blocks, one levels them and places cavity-ties. In the background, two are mixing, two barrowing mortar and blocks and another is cutting. Someone who has never laid blocks before can only lay a small number in a day, but in a team like this, work can really shoot ahead. The children, of course, laid bricks, not heavy blocks. They also used to like to help at the end of school, before the journey home, so we used to keep simple nailing and other such jobs ready for them.

With the inefficiency lessons of renovating the main school behind us, we tried to manage the work-site effectively. To minimize damage to the place, and to its mood and spirit, we kept all building materials within the building and courtyard perimeter, clearing only another three to five feet for working space. This allowed us to get to know the sunlight and shade throughout day and year. When eventually we were ready to open up the site for more sunlight, we knew which trees needed to be felled, and which only pruned. Some lank saplings we bent down and laced together to form green 'bowers'. We used the slope to our advantage, placing stores where they only needed to move downhill, if at all. Most could be crane-delivered to point of use. This saved endless slog - I wish I had done this in earlier buildings I had built.

Another lesson learnt from Nant-y-Cwm was that any design on paper could always be improved on the spot - indeed many junctions of shape and form could never be adequately pre-visualised. We mocked up options for window positions, ceiling shapes, door arch angles and the like, by tacking up battens or holding plasterboard scraps, then decided by consensus. This increased heart involvement of all concerned, but it did have an unanticipated side-effect. One or two individuals interpreted it as an invitation to insert their own preferences, regardless of the overall underlying intentions, or of anyone else. This led to difficult personal situations and the physical legacy of two paths: one, winding to hug the slope edge with the intriguing invitation of unfolding views, was three-quarter finished when its successor cut like an arrow through vegetation and obstacles. Nonetheless, this process of fine-tuning the design out of listening to the actual, developing situation added immeasurably to the quality of what we built. The life of the social process and the enrichment of those involved leave a lasting imprint in the spirit that the building emanates.

Chapter 4
Nant-y-Cwm Steiner Kindergarten

The starting point of the design was to look at the state of being of children between four and six-and-a-half years old, and at how Steiner education and the whole school-day experience relate to this.

Children at this age have no defences. They absorb - and imitate - everything around them. As they are so open to the qualities and messages of their surroundings, an underlying requirement for any building for small children is that it is harmonious and gentle, has a 'life' to its forms, spaces, textures, colours, light, materials and so on, and that it is as magical and full of reverent wonder as an ancient fairy tale.

Children's play is led in one or other direction by outer circumstances. These may be random, but at school are consciously directed. Hence the circular classrooms, but as circles are such unambiguous and therefore lifeless shapes, they are only hinted at, never completely defined. Arcs of wall, conical ceilings and centred flooring pattern reinforce the sense of circular enclosure, although the circle itself is never complete. These socially unifying spaces are balanced by the corner nooks into which children like to disperse during free play; like behind-the-sofa and under-the-table spaces at home, these are the places children seek as 'houses' for the worlds they construct in their imagination.

Those 'nooks' are in the form of soft-cornered play alcoves, with coloured glass windows. Different colours evoke different moods - in adults as well as children. The light through coloured glass gives each alcove a mood quite distinct from the main social space. In some alcoves there are two or three windows of different colours so that an interplay of coloured light is created, varying with sun position and strength.

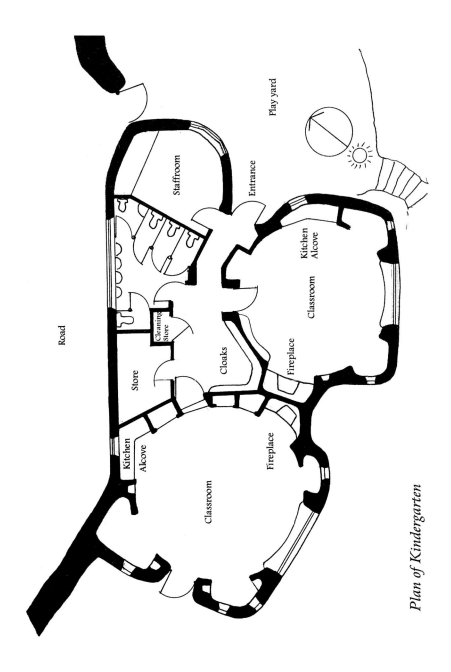

Road

Kitchen
Alcove

Classroom

Fireplace

Store

Cleaning
Store

Cloaks

Fireplace

Classroom

Kitchen
Alcove

Staffroom

Entrance

Play yard

Plan of Kindergarten

One alcove in each classroom is a child-scaled kitchen.

In the classrooms, the mood is one of secure calm warmth - activity-inducing in a gentle, dreamy way. The colour is pink. As the rooms are Lazure painted, it is the colour of the light that sets the mood. This technique is used throughout the building to enliven the interplay of formed surface, texture, colour and light.

As light from windows in different walls has so much more life than mono-directional light we sought this wherever possible. Wall texture, as well as differentially absorbing pigment and reflecting light, also softens the light-modelling and, along with the airy and unmaterial quality of Lazure painting, gives the boundaries of space a sort of 'life', making them feel more permeable, less confrontingly imprisoning.

With children's health in mind, we naturally chose non-toxic materials wherever possible. We also sought actually to stimulate life. This needs artistic measures. Throughout the building, from classrooms to toilets, light, texture and form gently stimulate the senses, so nourishing sense-linked organs like the pituitary and pineal glands. Qualities of line, shape and form are specifically chosen for gentle energizing effects.

Small children, their bodies still forming, their state of soul a reflection of the experiences around them, need to live with one foot in the world of imagination. Straight lines, and the harshness, imposed organization and imagination restriction that these bring are harmful. Support for life-energies is important for children at this age, as much energy is still going into building up their bodies. Curves, however, always risk allowing excessive indulgence; they can be too free, too un-earth-anchored-fantastic. I have sought a balance by controlling curves in three ways: some are arcs of the classroom circle; some are built up out of straight lines (literally, with concrete blocks or plasterboard sheet) so that they have some of the firmness of the straight within them; and thirdly there are those modelled from render or plaster, sculpturally firm, since they have within them invisible form-giving forces, such as gravity, thrust, implied movement and gesture, which support the form-giving process that the children's bodies and souls are going through. In this building, straight lines have within them a hint of the life-enhancing quality of the curve. Indeed many are faintly curved; others have to depend on texture or elusive surface veil colour to achieve this quality.

The site slopes between a minor road and a river, and had been planted with conifers. Apparently untouched for thirty years, these were now interspersed with lanky deciduous

The kindergarten grows at the point where the roadside hedge-bank accelerates into a bend. This growth-point energy is transformed and raised into a building.

The rear of the kindergarten forms enclosing suntrap nooks, making it more a boundary of outdoor space than building as object. Both how the building is placed and the way its base flares to root it into the ground help anchor it inevitably into place.

seedlings. Unmanaged and unkempt, it had nonetheless developed a spirit, full of life energy, evident everywhere - from moss and ivy-covered stumps to bird-rich canopy. The river is shallow and swift-flowing. Its song and glittering reflections bring a special mood. Though the road is little more than a twisting woodland lane, only occasionally disturbed by vehicles, it is not a place for small children.

Into this context we sought to fit the kindergarten, entirely new building as it would be, as inevitably as though it had always been there. Placed along the road edge, it shields the 'child-world' magic grove from occasional passing traffic, as well as freeing as much land as possible. The building is less an object than the hard boundary of a soft outdoor room. To anchor it into the place, it grows out of the boundary hedge at the point the road turns a bend. To root the building durably into the ground, the walls flare at the base and the ground surfaces sweep up to them.

Although the building needed to fit inevitably and unobtrusively into place, we did not want it to be excessively self-effacing or camouflaged. Such an approach could give out messages of guilt and deceit - not what is needed as a foundation for life! Rather than a stone finish, we chose therefore to build in blockwork with its external render finish Lazured with a warm earth colour limewash. The singing line of the fascia, generated by the interaction of the conical classroom roofs and the round-cornered, semi-rectangular plan, is given prominence by blue-green stain.

Young children breathe the world around them; what they experience, they express. Aggressive surroundings breed aggressive play, harmonious ones, harmonious play. What do they experience here? The process of arrival at the building is intended to support a transformation of the child's inner state-of-being.

From car-park to classroom - both outer (physical) and inner preparatory journey. From tree-arch through woodland path, portal, play-yard, narrow entrance and passage, golden cloak-lobby, classroom thresholds to the rooms themselves, the space, gestures, light, colour and mood continually expand and contract.

Almost all children come to school by car. Car journeys are kaleidoscopically visually stimulated with little link-up with the other senses. Moreover lift sharing usually means that as many children are stuffed into a car as will fit. Thus the journey is usually overcrowded, hurried and fractious. When car doors open, children are more likely to run, shout and push, than be the little angels we would like them to be. They need to leave the aggressive over-stimulating vehicular world behind them so as to be ready to enter into the mood of quiet wonder appropriate to a Steiner kindergarten. So we take them for a walk along about a hundred metres of twisting woodland path. In the process, they cross several thresholds: first a leaf archway; then a sun-dappled cliff edge above the shining, singing river; then shady woodland. The path finishes with an uphill slope. This brings you more into yourself, whereas a downhill one would do the reverse: children (and even some adults) would break into a run. As they pass under an overhanging roof 'archway' and pivot past the firewood shed, they see for the first time their destination. The boundary gate opens to a sunlit brick play-yard with sand-heap - the first stopping place on the journey. Here they see the entrance - invitingly gestured. Unlike fascistic post-modern forceful-axis design, this is deliberately slightly asymmetrical to invite, not compel. Inside there is a bluish passage, low, twisting, and darker. The blue quietens the children (and brings them more into themselves). The colour actually subtly moves from purplish to greenish-blue, so the infusion of warmth, then light, softens the transition from the earth-red exterior to the sunlit golden space to which the passage leads. This is a second stopping place. Here they leave behind their outdoor clothes and muddy boots - and the outdoor mood these carry with them. They are now ready to enter the classroom.

To do so they must pass through a portal confirmed through at least six senses. The archway is deep and the door substantial, though not too heavy for children. The wooden latch feels, moves and sounds solidly. The floor surface changes from hard quarry tiles to softer wood. One must change direction and also level. To one classroom there are steps; the other, though at the same level has, due to the sloping ground, windows looking into treetops, so feels like an upper storey. The colour now is rose and the classroom always seasonally decorated, perhaps with a blazing fire in the grate. Its gentle light, smells and warmth are different to all that has gone before. After a linear journey, the child is now in a circular space with a rising ceiling - a place to stop and to be in.

Each of these changes marks a step in leaving one world behind and preparing oneself inwardly for a new one: leaving chaotic, sensorially unbalanced over-stimulation and stepping into a socially harmonious, wonder-filled, quiet, stable security - a magical world.

Chapter 5
How we did things:
Details of Construction

Nant-y-Cwm Kindergarten is quite conventional in construction, but not everyone believes this, so I am frequently asked how we made various bits of it. For the practically minded, therefore, I'll describe some of the less conventional variants on conventional construction:

<u>Setting-out</u>

This was not easy. The site had obstructions, like huge tree stumps, too large to remove except by excavator - which, for cost reasons, would not come till after marking out. It sloped, so measurements had to be taken on the level and plumbed down. The only feature we were sure would not be destroyed in excavation was a telegraph pole. In this, we drove a nail, one metre above floor level. From this, we could set up a baseline, and from this find the classroom circle centres by triangulation. Everything else could now be located either by triangulation or gridded using a large three-four-five triangle. For excavation, curves were rationalised to straight lines to suit a JCB's straight-line bucket draw. These we reduced with shuttering boards or enlarged by hand to get the shapes needed. Thereafter, everything could be found by the earlier triangulation, grid or offset off straight-lines method.

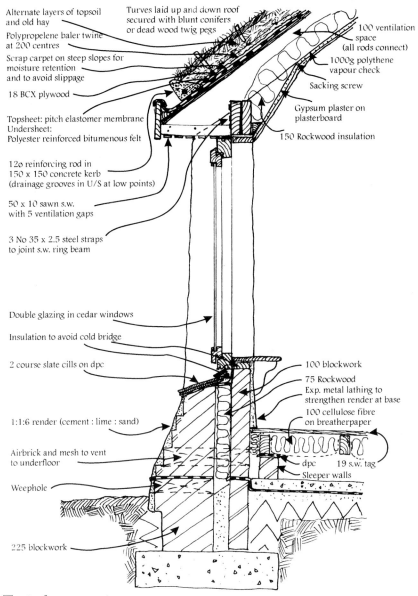

Alternate layers of topsoil
and old hay

Polypropelene baler twine
at 200 centres

Scrap carpet on steep slopes for
moisture retention
and to avoid slippage

18 BCX plywood

Topsheet: pitch elastomer membrane
Undersheet:
Polyester reinforced bitumenous felt

12ø reinforcing rod in
150 x 150 concrete kerb
(drainage grooves in U/S at low points)

50 x 10 sawn s.w.
with 5 ventilation gaps

3 No 35 x 2.5 steel straps
to joint s.w. ring beam

Double glazing in cedar windows

Insulation to avoid cold bridge

2 course slate cills on dpc

1:1:6 render (cement : lime : sand)

Airbrick and mesh to vent
to underfloor

Weephole

225 blockwork

Turves laid up and down roof
secured with blunt conifers
or dead wood twig pegs

100 ventilation
space
(all rods connect)

1000g polythene
vapour check

Sacking screw

Gypsum plaster on
plasterboard

150 Rockwood insulation

100 blockwork

75 Rockwood
Exp. metal lathing to
strengthen render at base

100 cellulose fibre
on breatherpaper

dpc   19 s.w. tag

Sleeper walls

Typical construction.

37

Walls

These are all brick or block. Tight curves and walls below damp-proof course level are brickwork, everything else concrete block - locally made and much cheaper in this area. The outer walls are of cavity construction, but the inner and outer leaves follow room and building shape respectively, resulting in a variable width cavity. This is sometimes too wide for ties, but the curvature of the wall gives stability. These walls are insulated with 75mm rockwool batts. In the over-wide cavities, these are held in place by bent ties with horizontal rockwool 'shelves' in places to restrict convection in the cavity.

The Roof

This is a timber structure with a plywood deck. The roadside roof was simple; less so the circular classrooms. Here, the ring-beam is rationalised into straight-line segments. These were connected by perforated steel straps, fixed by 6" nails slipped through holes drilled through the timber and then clenched tight. With twenty nails per strap and three straps per joint, this was laborious but still simpler than trying to match exact-angled steel plates, every angle different, due to different segment lengths, with inexact site conditions. It rained almost continually during this stage, so drill-bits jammed in wet wood and electric tools were dangerous to use.

We then set up a scaffold tower at the centre and mounted the plywood cap disc (edged and cross-braced with 100mm timber) at the right level. A plumb-bob hung from its centre located it over the centre-nail in the concrete below. From this nail, we could measure how much closer or further out from the notional circle each rafter end was and so calculate how much higher or lower its seat should be.

As the circle was unevenly faceted, every rafter was a different length, so each one had to be set in place on blocks to get the right slope, for in-situ marking. Rafters over the corner alcoves were merely laid from ring to props on the unfinished wall, plumbed down and notched to bear on the brickwork. Their built-in ends were DPC wrapped. After the two classroom cones and the simple-plane roof along the roadside were framed, the bridging shapes between were obvious - it was just a matter of joining up the gaps.

This was not the end of challenging carpentry! To clad cones in ply is not as straightforward as might be imagined. Our system was to fix all the easy sheets - the simple planes - first, then the cone. With a bevel-square, we marked the angle at which each new sheet would meet the previous one and cut it off before lifting onto the roof. We then put this sheet in place, securely nailed its junction edge and sprung it down across the curve - usually by lying on it, then clamping down. Now we could nail it to all but its last rafter, mark this one central on the rafter, release the clamps and cut it with a power saw, the blade set only one millimetre deeper than the ply thickness. These vicious tools must *always* be held with both hands, lest the blade snag, bouncing the saw unpredictably. I didn't know this at the time; only luck kept us amputation-free. I have since learnt that someone with only nine fingers is usually a carpenter.

Roof Waterproofing Membrane:

This I had adamantly refused to undertake with volunteers as I felt it too critical an element to make mistakes on, and well beyond our skills. In the event, shortage of money forced us to choose between doing it ourselves or watching the building rot.

Shaping the roof.

Shaping the roof (continued).

We chose cold adhesive jointing compound as I was apprehensive of slopping hot tar buckets into Wellington boots, high on an unprotected roof. We used a pitch co-polymer capsheet over polyester-reinforced, high-performance bitumenous-felt. Not very desirable environmentally, but the best we could get at that time.

Turf Roof

Onto the waterproof membrane we laid scrap synthetic carpet, collected from skips, to protect it from damage, and also to retain moisture - as it does so well after burst pipes. The carpet stuck to the bitumen our poor workmanship had over-spread at every membrane overlap, giving us a non-slip surface in place of the greasy-smooth capsheet. A welcome bonus on a 38° roof!

Continuously along the eaves, we cast in-situ a reinforced concrete curb. This had polypropylene twine (baler-twine) loops protruding which we laced together over the ridge and to rope rings around the cone tops. These up and down strings we tensioned by deforming them to zig-zags with horizontal ties. Under all this, we stuffed spoiled hay, then with a bucket chain the Swedish teenagers covered it with topsoil. Then more hay, more soil and so on until we had used it all up. By calculation this should have given 150mm of earth over the whole roof, and did in fact, fill the whole curb depth. In places we added more earth to subtly sculpt the roof shape. The actual effect is that the grass grows longer here, exaggerating our intention.

We then unrolled turves up and down the roof, pegging them down with short blunt coniferous or dead deciduous twigs to avoid the mistake on my first turf roof. Here, I used ash pegs: they all sprouted into little trees - with tough membrane penetrating roots. Between turves, we planted wildflowers, but with roofing euphoria over and other tasks more pressing, unfortunately not enough.

The woodshed roof was simpler and cheaper. On the site-felled pole structure, we nailed joists at 450mm centres for extra strong support for corrugated fibre-cement sheeting. Due to gale damage across Britain, there was an eight month wait for deep corrugation sheets so we had to use shallow profile ones. On this was spread doubled 2000 gauge · polythene topped with hay and 150 mm soil as before. As the slope was shallow enough for soil not to wash off, we just seeded this with hayshed sweepings and wildflower seeds. As soil-retaining curbs, we used site-cut spruce logs tied together with baler twine. By the time they have rotted, the root mat, enmeshed with the twine, should adequately hold the soil together.

Shaping the Ceilings

Plasterboard is easy to shape by bending, folding or faceting. Three-dimensional curves need expanded-metal-lathing. We trapped razor-sharp cut-edges under adjoining plasterboard so as not to slice fingers during hand-finishing.

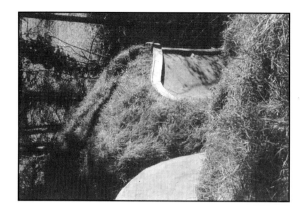

Shaping a corner alcove.

Hand-finished Plastering

On brick and blockwork, we used lime-rich render: 9:2:1 (sand : lime : cement) externally, 10:2½:⅔ internally. The technique is to dampen the wall, sweep the floor clean so you can use the droppings, and apply with a non-rectangular tool. My favourite is a round-nosed bricklaying trowel. With two trowels, one big, one small (called a 'gauging trowel'), you can fill-in or cover-over corners and also use one trowel to press the other tight to the wall. Some people prefer to just use rubber gloves. I aim, at this stage, for three-dimensional undulations without deep trowel marks, and a slight taper from the base to enhance solidity.

The rate at which a wall sucks moisture from the render depends on its material, dryness and atmospheric conditions. It is usually around three-quarters of an hour till the surface is stiff enough to rub to its final form with rubber-gloved hands. Do this too soon and finger scrapes will show, also over-thick patches will sweat moisture to the surface and slump. Too late and the rubbed surface will be sandy and scratched. Unlike gypsum plaster, which grants only a few minutes tolerance, it is quite easy to find the right time to rub lime render. The aim is to achieve a surface that undulates unostentatiously, full of the life imprinted by the hands, but without the contrivance of tool or finger marks. And hands do indeed imprint life: as a massage therapist told me during a hand-plastering course: "there is no part of the human body that the human hand is not shaped to fit." With such a technique, we massage the physical sheath around us. Moreover, hands are vehicles for care and sensitivity. Indeed you cannot make non-repetitive things by hand without engaging these feelings - and these in turn radiate onto those who inhabit rooms so made.

Expanded-metal-lathing won't hold much render, so just wipe it over with the first mix. Next day it will easily take 80% coverage and by the next is easy to finish. Try to do it all at once and just as you have almost finished, the whole lot will peel away - in my experience, invariably falling inside my shirt. The same principle applies with gypsum plaster but its rapid set means the only limitation is to do the job in three stages.

Lime is not compatible with gypsum so plasterboard needs gypsum plaster. This sets fast, especially in improperly cleaned buckets with old mix residues. Timing is much more crucial than with render. Plaster is rather smooth grain, so the finishing coat was 1 sand to 4 plaster, brushed on as a slurry and wet-brushed to finish.

Lazure Painting

In this technique, light is reflected off a textured white base through thin veils of colour, infusing the space with a mood of coloured light. Beeswax based paints are durable, washable but expensive; water-based paints are cheaper. I advise non-toxic paints - and certainly *never* masonry paints, which contain mercuric fungicide. We used casein-based white emulsion and veils of Stockmeyer and Windsor & Newton artists' watercolour, so dilute that you could only just see the colour when wet on the wall, and not at all when dry. Yet to step into a room with even only a single invisible veil, was to unmistakably breathe the colour, and to step out of it was to feel other rooms, still white, just cold and sterile. You can hardly make veils too weak - it just means more work and longer drying out; but too strong and you risk having to paint everything white to start again. Unless really experienced with colour, I always recommend starting with warm colours, much as preparing water-colour paper for a summery mood. Start with a blue veil and you may never be able to warm it up.

Techniques vary. You can use sponges or brushes, several veils of one colour (the texture picks up different density from each veil) or different hues over each other. We used 6" brushes with generous dancing strokes, and brushed out as dry as possible. Absolutely essential is that someone stays around at the end of work to brush out any runs, otherwise you will be greeted on the morrow by a wall of regency stripes.

The classrooms are veiled with rose madder, alizarin crimson and ultramarine blue, with, in selected places, vermilion - three to five veils. The passage, alizarin crimson faded into yellow under ultramarine blue; the coat-lobby, yellow, yellow-ochre and vermilion; and the staff-room, yellow, yellow-ochre and ultramarine.

One consequence of using natural paints is that many visitors comment on the beautiful scent. While ambient smell, like background sound (in this case, the river), quickly becomes so taken-for-granted that it disappears from notice, it continues to influence mood. What we had chosen merely for non-toxicity, turned out to more deeply nourishing.

Finishes on Wood

Exterior timber was finished with deck-oil ('dekkolja'). On the sawn-wood fascia, structural windows and cover-boards over joinery joints, this had artists' oil-paint pigment mixed in. Cedar windows and doors were uncoloured, just oiled. Interior sawn wood was painted with egg-oil emulsion.

This is mixed in equal measures - i.e. one egg shell: egg, boiled linseed oil, and water, with a few drops of pure turpentine (or peppermint or lavender oil) to prevent the egg rotting. Into this are mixed powder pigments: zinc white (translucent) for the first coat, then other colours in translucent veils. Try to use a single dry brush-stroke along the grain so that its texture shows through. Leave twelve to twenty-four hours between veils, so the paint is still tacky, not glossy dry.

All other interior woodwork was treated with boiled linseed oil. Beware of linseed oil rags. They can self-ignite and so must be put outside after use. I know of two schools burnt down by such fires. For floors we used a beeswax, carnauba wax and linseed oil mixture, but it was not satisfactory. Better to buy a low-toxic solvent beeswax formulation.

Exterior Wall Paint

This was a centuries-old formula. Lime and a small amount of protein was added to water and stirred daily for at least a week. All traditional recipes recommend a cat, but we used meat instead. Blood or urine can also be used but we had no volunteers to bleed or pee in public. The clear alkaline fluid was then ladled out, mixed with earth colours, some of which we dug nearby, and applied in about five thin veils. This is akin to the material nature makes stalagmites out of. Unfortunately this recipe started a (groundless) rumour that we sacrificed cats to appease the Gods of building.

Duration and Cost

All in all the kindergarten cost some £36 000 and took three years to build. Why so much and so long? Most materials were new, only some were secondhand. In a few places we were able to use poles cut from the trees we had had to fell. To put the price in perspective, contract cost would probably have been three times as much.

Except for workshop courses, most work was on a one day a week basis, school hours only - the maximum that most volunteers would come for and the majority of these were unskilled. Volunteer work is anyway unpredictable, but the slow completion was largely due to inefficiencies forced by the shoestring budget. Cash-flow interruptions meant repeated stops and starts - making it hard to maintain volunteer enthusiasm. It also caused mismatch of work and season so that outdoor work was unavoidable in winter, leaving indoor work for summer. This, I estimated, added half to one year.

But the slow pace of work also had a benefit. It allowed us to really get to know the place and the building so that we could continually fine tune and improve on the design as work proceeded. Despite all the problems, gift-work imparts a harmonious, non-aggressive mood to the building site and leaves an imprint in the finished building, enspiriting it. And anyway, slow or not, we were able to build a kindergarten which, had we waited till all the money was there or opted not to use volunteers, would still be just a dream.

Chapter 6
From Past to Future

In 1990 the kindergarten was finished. Not exactly *finished*, but sufficiently so for teachers and children to move in. What a relief! But life doesn't stop with completed buildings. How they are used, as distinct from how we had *anticipated* they would be used, makes new demands and teaches new lessons. And children grow; that which suits infants will not necessarily be appropriate to older children.

What lessons has the kindergarten taught us? What, therefore, would I do differently next time? What new needs do older children have? And so what sort of buildings suit them?

Should it have been larger? Yes - you can always reduce perceived space if need be. Nine-inch shelves all around a classroom would make it seem 20% smaller. Should there have been three classrooms? In many Waldorf schools one third of the kindergarten children go on to Class One each year, so three kindergarten classrooms would be the right number. But all such increases in size cost money, time and energy. None were in surplus. Although at around £36,000, the kindergarten cost only a fifth of comparable buildings, this sum was a crippling burden for many years.[1]

Then there is the matter of scale. The kindergarten teachers who briefed me asked for infant scaled fittings. But the child-low kitchen counters are also used by teachers and are

[1] Mark Dudek in Kindergarten Architecture (Spon London 1996) compares a London kindergarten costing £1440 per sq. metre with Nant-y-cwm at around £290 per sq. metre.

hard on adult backs. One way to overcome this is by peninsular counters with a sunken floor one side, so making it both adult and child height. This takes more space of course and is not disabled accessible.

Places precisely designed for one particular purpose don't adapt to new use so easily. The (materially) 'functional' buildings of recent decades have proved much less readily adaptable than older buildings with less specifically allocated spaces. This brings up a conflict between spiritual functionalism and flexibility to meet unknown future needs. Nevertheless, so many people have wanted the kindergarten as a house, that it seems it would easily accommodate such a use - and it has already been used for conferences.

In only a few years, several specifically designed spaces found new uses that they were not designed for. The kindergarten opened with play 'caves' , sunk about four feet below floor level, balustraded and gated for safety. Play lofts seem successful in other schools, but I did not allow for two factors. Most are for six to seven year-old children. Four to six year-olds are a lot younger. and children push to get in. Whereas upwards is only a few rungs to push up, downwards mean they can push each other off the ladder. Moreover, the sea of soft cushions envisaged at the bottom never happened. These alcoves were subsequently floored over. So was a shallow one, not for safety, but to increase the general floor area, though at the price of multi-level play opportunities. Other smaller and more temporary changes included using the staff-room first for music tuition then as a kitchen. Designed for meetings and class preparation, with a couch doubling as sick-bed, it had no extract ventilation, water or wipe-down surfaces. Play nooks became cupboards, while cupboards had doors removed for playing in. How much of this should I have anticipated and designed for?

Another problem is noise. It is well known that circular rooms focus sound at the centre, but how much do textured surfaces and walls broken up by alcoves and shelves compensate for this? I overestimated this effect, but even though the empty building focussed sound slightly, I was confident that cushions, rugs and soft furnishings would absorb it sufficiently. Yet beyond a central carpet, there never were any. And when one classroom became a messy activities room, even the carpet went. Also children are much noisier than carpenters!

What would I do differently next time? There *is* a fundamental conflict between needs of space and acoustics. Socially focussing spaces also focus noise - and the better they do one, the better the other. More coarsely textured plaster would help, but not much. Other ceiling materials, like woodwool, cork or fibre-board would require a faceted ceiling. Timber boarding can allow discrete sound absorptive slots. But all these would visually harden the space. For unifying calm, they would need to be painted, which reduces sound absorption. Perhaps I would again rely on copious soft furnishings - after all, these are the main noise dampeners in most rooms. Wall hangings and hanging moss-filled discs, seasonally decorated would have to suffice in messy rooms.

All these problems highlight conflicting requirements and the difficulty of finding the appropriate balance points. To make it even more difficult, those balance points and priorities agreed during design may not be appropriate in practice. A lesson I am still digesting.

Another conflict of priorities occurs in the landscaping. My normal approach is to develop a place out of what is already there. This includes trees, shrubs and ground vegetation. But children play in a different way among light-filled trees like birch, or even hazel and ash, to the way in which they play among dark, heavy ones, like azalea and, to some extent, dense spruce or even sycamore in heavy summer leaf. There were plenty of spruces, quite a number of sycamore, a few ash and no birch. We pruned the lower branches off the spruce, lightening the heavy darkness - and letting in sunlight - but retaining the protective crown. All the other trees were small so it was possible to favour selected species and cut others back. This allows a gentle transition, over a period of time, from one mood to another.

But what of the children's transition as they move up through the school? What qualities should their surroundings manifest as they grow through childhood?

There are, of course, already classrooms in the main school building, but as pupil numbers grow, these are becoming too few and too small. At the time we built them, limited by the existing building shell and a minute budget, these small rooms were the only possible choice. New classrooms are urgently needed - but what should they be like? What do middle-school children need?

Like flowers, children grow into the light, needing it more and more, until as teenagers they start to sunbathe. They grow up in stature and increasing individualisation, especially of one group, or 'gang' from another. Also they start to want to *understand* things around them, and how they work. In this middle-school period, seven to fourteen years old, the polarities of life: good - bad, fair - unfair, become clearer and more important to them.

How do these translate into architectural qualities? Whereas small children live in a more dreamy world, at this age they need more sunlight. They need clearer, firmer spaces with upwardly posture-inductive gestures. They need to see how things stand up, how they work. And they need contrasting experiences: outside - inside, dark - light, constricted - spacious, and rhythmical patterns that can bring these polar experiences into a unifying relationship.

These qualities we have tried to embody in the new classroom proposals. They are sunny and generously high. Though twisting with life, the places are simpler to comprehend, even define - in contrast to the elusive, life-generated spaces of the kindergarten, only subtly unified by geometry. They are solar heated, of legible construction and with reed-bed grey water treatment. Small spaces contrast with large ones in breathing rhythm. A rhythm of subtle metamorphosis flows along the long, linear building, with the identity of each classroom distinct.

But how did we arrive at the form? Teachers, development group members and myself worked together. First we looked at what is already there, concentrating on the message the physical environment gives to newcomers. Disproportionately important, for first impressions make the foundation filter for how they will subsequently view the school. We therefore met in the car-park - the first arrival point - and walked the route that the children take to their classrooms. We tried to just absorb the experience, without judgement, evaluation, thought or response - and definitely without *ideas* of what to do. This is not as easy as it sounds.

This journey seemed to be made up of several distinct parts. Our thoroughness somewhat dampened by rain, we now divided into small groups to look at each of these, and the other distinct areas of school and playground, more methodically. Firstly, what exactly was there? This is the solely *physical* here and now. We then came together to share observations. Then we looked at movement and life. How do the sequence of spatial gestures and polar qualities of weight and levity, darkness and light flow into each other as we move along the route? Again, we shared our experiences, building a whole journey and a whole 'campus' from parts studied in detail, but separately. What then were the *moods* of different parts? Gloomy, messy, verdant, calm and so on. So what did the whole experience *say*? What was the subliminal message of the school and the land - one which would be 'read' by everybody?

But what *should* it say? The inner being of the school is all about care and nurture for children, but how can this be embodied in its physical substance? What moods of place would support this message? To integrate these, how should polar qualities and gestures be moderated or enhanced? In what sequence and with what character of flow should they relate to each other? What changes to what is already there would initiate such effects?

Having run similar workshops elsewhere, I was confident that small changes could effect disproportionately large transformations. This proved also to be the case here. The back-yard, for instance, has a forgotten air, an atmosphere of dereliction - a place to get up to mischief in. Using it as craft-workshop yard would both bring it back to life, making it a centre of attention, and could separate this noisy, working-mess zone from the main play area. This focuses the 'heart' of the playground more in the front. Moving the entrance and arching it with a rose pergola would further strengthen this. A cantilevered bay on an upstairs classroom, necessary for space, also makes a welcoming entrance porch.

Knowing the moods of the different areas, we asked ourselves where new activities - notably classrooms, hall and garden plots *asked* to be. Some locations just felt right.

Moreover, they substantiated the findings of our initial study. The playground 'heart' asks for further enclosure to contain and intensify it. This suggests the plan gesture with which the school should grow. The new playground entrance and the way it focuses view now suggests the location of the future hall - a building which, as a house for cultural activities for the whole school, both consolidates its spirit and, through plays and the like, is a contact point with the outer world.

Now things seemed to fall into place. The long arm of classrooms is ideally oriented for morning solar heating - a perfect match to occupation time. The face of the building into the courtyard asked to be cloakrooms and passage. These make a spatial buffer - and also a thermal one, for overheating or chill is less critical here.

By now, we had walked around and envisaged the extent and line of the future building. It was easy to draw a plan of this. But what would it look like? It was time to model in clay.

After a few trials of different forms, within an hour or two we had a consensus design. The building form was unified, but each classroom individualized by its own entrance. It would be economically simple to construct, but alive and welcoming. Even the problems of phasing a unified building could be overcome. All now to be done was to be precise about sizes, refine details and draw it up. This is now done. Now all that remains is to build it. In this case, for speed reasons, partly with contractors, partly volunteers.

And then, perhaps, I really can put building Nant-y-Cwm Steiner school behind me. Or...?

Proposed hall and classrooms. These emphasize legibility of their underlying form-giving principles: construction is framed with local roundwood poles; life-support systems like solar heating and reedbed grey-water treatment are fully visible; and the new grows out of the old, consolidating its latent place-enclosing gesture.

Proposed New Building : South Elevation

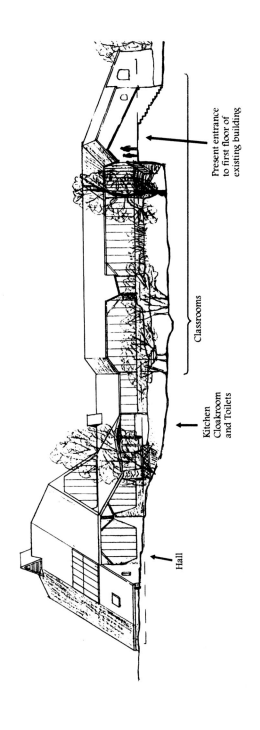

Present entrance
to first floor of
existing building

Classrooms

Kitchen
Cloakroom
and Toilets

Hall

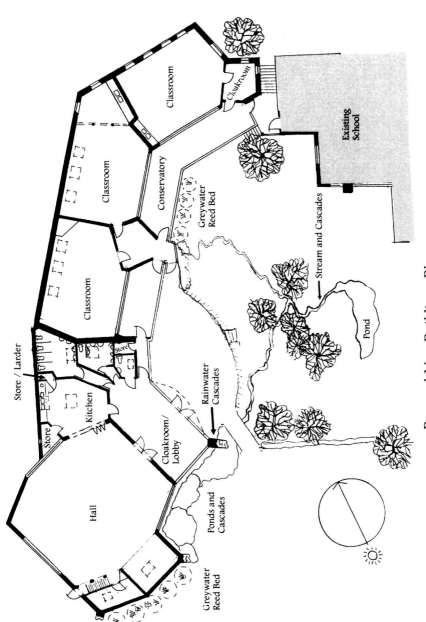

Proposed New Building : Plan

Christopher Day is also author of:

PLACES OF THE SOUL: Architecture and Environmental Design as a Healing Art (Thorsons: Harper Collins 1990)

BUILDING WITH HEART: A Practical Approach to Self and Community Building (Green Books 1990)

If you have enjoyed this book you may be interested in these other titles published by Starborn Books:

PETER'S BOOK OF ROUNDS:
A collection of new rounds and canons,
composed by Peter Oram and illustrated by Phil Forder.
ISBN 1 899530 00 2   Price £5.00

SEVEN STARS OF GOLD:
A collection of poems for children, written by Peter Oram
and illustrated by Phil Forder.
ISBN 1 899530 01 0   Price £5.00

THE MIDNIGHT TRAIL:
A Christmas story for children, written by Phil Forder
and Peter Oram, with illustrations by Phil Forder.
ISBN 1 899530 02 9   Price £5.00

THE ENCIRCLED CROSS:
Tales of the Saints of Pembrokeshire and the Gower,
written by Phil Forder and Peter Oram,
with illustrations by Phil Forder.
ISBN 1 899530 03 7   Price £5.00

ONE FOR THE GOLDEN SUN:
A new collection of pentatonic songs for young children,
many with simple instrumental accompaniments.
Composed by Peter Oram with illustrations by Phil Forder.
ISBN 1 899530 04 5   Price £5.00

All the above books are obtainable through your local bookshop, or else may be ordered direct from Starborn Books at the address shown on the reverse of the title page of this book. Also available from the same address and written by the same authors, but published by the Pädagogische Forschungsstelle beim Bund der freien Waldorfschulen, Stuttgart, is an earlier collection of pentatonic children's songs, **A CHANGE IN THE YEAR.**